PIECES OF THE JOURNEY – A COLLECTION

Other Books by Don Davison
An Outline of a Philosophy of the Consciousness of Truth
The Concept of Personhood in the Evolutionary Process of Being
The Game of Life: A Player's Manual for Executives and Others
Sign Posts: A Collection of Essays, Vol. I
Sign Posts: A Collection of Essays, Vol. II
Sign Posts: A Collection of Essays, Vol. III

Poetry
Thoughts and Feelings Book I
Thoughts and Feelings Book II
Needles from the Ponderosas at Zirahuen
Seeds from the Ponderosas at Zirahuen
Pitch from the Ponderosas at Zirahuen
Humus from the Ponderosas at Zirahuen
Sawdust from the Ponderosas at Zirahuen
Sun's rays through the Ponderosas at Zirahuen
Shadows beneath the Ponderosas at Zirahuen
Cones from the Ponderosas at Zirahuen
Pollen sifting from the Ponderosas at Zirahuen
Reflections from Lucerne
Searching Swamps
Questions
Time's Echoes
Memories

Collections
Always Extolling
Murmurings
Iris and Other Things
Through the Swamps of Time

PIECES OF THE JOURNEY – A COLLECTION

Don Davison

Zirahuen
Phoenix, AZ
pathtotheself.com
DrDavison@pathtotheself.com

©2010 by Zirahuen
All rights reserved
Printed in the United States of America

ISBN 978-0-9774039-9-8

No part of this book may be used or reproduced in any manner whatsoever without written permission except in the case of brief quotations embodied in critical articles and reviews.

Cover photo Don Davison
Author photo Patricia Davison

Special thanks to Louella Holter, formerly with the Bilby Research Center of Northern Arizona University, and to Tina Rosio, from W.

CONTENTS

Tree	1
Duty	2
Public vs. Private	3
Tasha	4
The Apple	6
The Hunt	7
The Storm	8
The Task	9
Just a Thought	10
To Pray	11
To Stop Time	12
Who	13
Winter	14
Bravery	16
Clearing the Land	17
Wanting	21
Diaspora	23
Cave	24
Him	25
Piece of Wood	27
To Embody	29
Heaven Sent	30
The Suckling	32
Mill	33
The Path	36
To One	38
Just Lava	39

Just One	40
Light	41
From the Mouth of the Cave	42
Worship	43
Me	44
Your Whisper	45
Snowflake I	46
Snowflake II	47
A Breath	48
A Conversation	49
A Glance	51
Almost…	52
As If...	53
Before and After	54
The Brass Ring	55
Cabin Logs	57
Children	58
Fall	60
Hey Mom! Hey Dad!	62
Self Portrait	63
Questions	65
Cities	66
A Distant Dream	67
Thoughts in a Hotel Room	69
Invasions	70
Life Given	71
Man	72
Petro!	73
For Reefus – Moments in the Life of a Fish and a Boy	74
The Wind	81
A Symphony	82
Technology	83
Tired Parent	84

Who are They?	85
Dragons	86
The Swamp	87
Monarchs	90
My Last Wonder	93
Juan de Aragon	94
The Bridge	119

All of Don Davison's books have water on their covers. Water is one of the most essential attributes of the planet Earth; without it, life as we know it would not exist. It deserves our most considered attention.

Davison's collections of poetry all end with "Finding Pieces." Many of you have asked, where did the rules for the Game of Life come from? They come from many places and different times. Good hunting!

To Patricia, for everything.

TREE

Leaves lost, torn by wind and hail.
What trail is left, where to the Holy Grail?
Abscission layers forming early,
leaving scars to hold and last the season.
Is there a plan in the pain of change,
does it harbor any reason?
Warm days sapped the moisture from the leaves.
The hue of the bark gives a hint to why it grieves.
Just to seed one other self
was the only desired gift.
"To be or not to be,"
is the chasm of being that forms the eternal rift.
The purpose is salvation,
the perpetuation of the kind.
Does one dying example
deny the grandeur of the mind?
Life and the changes of the years,
too fast, not enough time
to build the strength to win
when one is past his prime.
The tree is dead, the chapter done,
and now I know,
soon I too will lie
beneath the blanket of the snow.
P.S.
As I sweat in my chosen arenas,
I hear a shout,
"Maybe that is all you're here for –
to seed a son and die!"

DUTY

And then I saw it –
a final notice on the last page of the inside section,
"Flags at Half-Mast for Commandos."
Such a sense of national pride!

PUBLIC VS. PRIVATE

As I ran along a public road
and through a public park,
I marveled at a public lake
and heard a public concert.
I continued on through a public school yard
and across a public golf course.
I topped a rise and gazed across a panorama
of public streets and public housing projects
to the view beyond:
A public forest and a setting of the sun.
I asked myself
if there was something more that one needed
and suddenly a spark spit forth and seeded
a train of thought that ultimately did concede:
If there hadn't been a private purpose,
I would have difficulty
enjoying my public now.

TASHA

From still, dark, cold stretches of space
comes pregnant being through eons.
Then mega and giga volts split bonds
breaking a seeming stagnant stalemate.
Clouds of primeval dust,
scattered in the solar winds,
bend in time dropping to sight,
coalesced from chaos
and brought to life through light.
Rocks possess a hardness
and here and there
calcareous cemented sandstone
separates the layers.
Explosive energies
form in their destructive creativity
successive stages,
scourging flesh from bone,
giving birth to spirit in stripping life from stone.
And finally,
from a universe
life congeals
to let evolve a soft conglomerate of matter
that shares its spark of time with me.
My wife,
her warmth and strength,
from deep space in voids
between the quarks and leptons
there comes an energy of Love,
pulling progressive and ascendant
all that is and will become.
The only reason for being
is to fulfill
the internal and eternal master plan.

The wonder says to me,
"Here now is the fleeting vortex of the soul.
God sheds His grace on thee."
My arms encircle you
and in so doing capture space contained,
occupied now with your presence.
How long before the wind?
A hollow space,
the presence gone,
and yet the flute maintains the song.
Abba,
hear the message of the music
and lend a body to the space
for strength that gives salvation.

THE APPLE

The smell of clean air,
a body disposed,
the quarry still sought,
a moment of hunger.
To taste the tartness, the whiteness,
the delectable juice mixed with pieces
covered with small brown cinnamon spots,
a bright red
slightly salted with anemic absences,
or a pale sheen fading into a lush green richness,
is to reap a magnificent moment of the harvest.
Too hard, just right,
the snap of freshness that sets taste buds
and nostrils to a glorious titillation.
The fruit gives birth to the realization
of a perfect time.
Yesterday would have been too soon,
tomorrow too late.
The sky is clear.
The wind is gentle.
The disposition is so perfect.
Thank you my love!
The wealth of the apple
extends far beyond nutrition.

THE HUNT

To sit huddled in the warmth of woolen mittens
and stockings,
next to a hidden spring in mid-winter,
watching the wind whip tiny crystals
into sculptured forms of rivers,
valleys, and mountains,
is to sense the preciousness of being.
These are the yearning times
when incidents create a memory flow
that takes one back to those moments long ago.
It is to be that carrier of effervescent information
when we periodically,
in hidden silence,
experience subjugation.

THE STORM

We huddle through the evening's glow
until the stillness of the dawn
wondering what winter weather
the season's storm will spawn.
When the light of day descends,
behold the message that God sends!
On shrugged shoulders
hangs the burden of the night,
saintly sentries standing shrouded
in majestic cloaks of white.
What is the message
that lies within their captivating plight?
There seems to be something special
held all within their sight.
The world is cleansed by a mighty deed.
What more can we ask,
what more do we need?
Our souls have been touched by witnessing
His love.
When will we accept the ALL from above?

THE TASK

Moments treasured, lingering still.
How difficult to know Thy Will.
I see and do with You in mind,
Could I do less and still be kind?
There are so many who need your love,
Show me the way, lead from above.
I know so little.
I have so much.
And yet,
I really need Your Loving Touch.
Give me the grace to work and be
in ways that foster friends for Thee.

JUST A THOUGHT

Remember...
the children are still singing and playing
in the dust of Biafra,
in the lawns of Liverpool,
in the mud of Montevideo,
in the brick streets of Birmingham,
in the waters of Shanghai.
Laughter lives well
in the young hearts of the world.

TO PRAY

In the name of Allah,
The Compassionate, The Merciful
receive the soul of your fallen warriors
knowing full well that divine justice
will see its way
through the battle.
Indeed, it is now that we all realize,
life
is a Holy Endeavor.
We will spend our moments
in participative preparation
for the continuance of Your Divine Plan.
Oh Compassionate, Oh Merciful,
be praised!
And as we turn and see the crescent hanging high,
finally,
we know that transformation is nigh.

TO STOP TIME

I love rocks
because they seem to have a permanence
that goes beyond the rush from Spring to Fall.
They have a pace that moves generations
through their seasons,
from gentle children to adults
and to births again of fellowmen.
I watch and feel
as the process gives and steals.
Can I touch again the winds of Summer?

WHO

The roar of the jet cannot penetrate
the silence of the moment.
Life is everything!
In one square meter of ground
there exists more life forms
than in an entire city of men.
Life is Oh so Grand!
Yet, where,
oh where my stand?
Where fresh water meets the salty seas,
the smell of thee and me.
Rotting grabs ...
Life's giving moments.
A row of seagulls stand guarding the shore.
Tell me,
who is chairman of the board?
The flow of the rivers,
pushed and pulled,
tells me of the omnipotence of
The Force.
To turn our vital essence to the wind
is to travel life's path
with the spirit of humankind.

WINTER

Has Fall felt the silent snap of death
as Summer's strength slips out of breath?
Are the heavy droplets in the wind
sealed in crystals,
salting the soft brown forest floor?
Do you scurry in from wicked winds
and quickly close the door?
Have you had that brilliant morning
when the reflection of the sun
startles you and makes you wonder
what is it you've won?
Do swirling gusts of flakes pile in eddied corners
where winds lose their treasures?
Is your nose pressed to the pane
as you peer at a mercury thread
wondering what it measures?
Was that first snowfall a moist and laden one
that stuck to every surface
covering the windward
in a cloak of mighty fluff?
Have your muscles ached
as you sought to clear the tracks
of that heavy frozen stuff?
Do you feel the bite of the wind
as it sends stinging gifts
scattering across the snowscape?
Are your mittened hands hiding your face
as you dart from deed to deed
seeking your escape?

Has the silence yet descended
that smothers creaking shadows in the afternoons
as daylight shifts so quickly into night?
Have you taken that moonlit walk
when diamonds dance so dazzling bright?
Are nostrils sticky with the season,
having lost their sensitivity to smell,
leaving you only sight and sound
with which to reason?
Were hours spent in rolling
crunching speckled balls?
Are tracks of the first frolic
sticking to the walls?
Did you stack them one upon the other
in a sequence large to small
and end up with a Frosty
who wasn't very tall?
Does the stillness of the winter
wrap you in its silent grace,
tingling your fingers and hardening your face?
Is a fire burning gently with flaming fingers
curling through birch and oak?
Are winter clothes hanging heavy on the hearth,
dripping spots of liquid crystals,
lost as steam rises from your cloak?
Tell me, is winter there?
Has it come with its darkness and its lightness,
with its stillness and its fury?
I would give so much to be there
for just a moment's time.
Quick, tell me, hurry!
Is winter there?

BRAVERY

Plans are so easily made ...
   late at night
on a full stomach.

CLEARING THE LAND

As the sun sets in the west
it pulls images from hearts and souls
and sets them in the future.
We emerge from the womb
to be impressed by
each and every thing that surrounds us.
The tastes, touch, sounds, smells, and sights
become a personal pallette from which we paint
the shapes of our desires
and ultimately our dreams.
A process is set in motion
that leads us through the present
carrying in our minds those
perfect states captured and held
as cherished possibilities.
Time passes and the edges of the images fade
in tones of deeds done and reality encountered.
Still,
as sunsets scatter homeward
the souls of us all,
the center of the picture burns bright
throughout the years.
There are those moments when we stop
and sense that now
… a perfect happening ...
longed for, dreamt about,
prayed for and wondered about
came to be.
A red head! A girl!
A whole new world flashes out before me,
a daughter now.

Soft shades of similarity from that first moment
– another angel –
no, not yet,
for now a cherub.
A ragged old sweatshirt and a rusty old red bike
form pictures of determination
blossoming into smiles as she says,
"Mom! Dad! Look! I can do it!"
So many things to learn.
So many things to try.
So many dreams to be fulfilled.
A daughter plays a piano as late afternoon
sunrays
sneak across the recital floor,
reminding us in their movement
of the effervescence of the process.
From gentle, small and cuddly,
the children moved so fast
from little men who "travel" nails
with miniature hammers
to silent shadows that watch the world unfold.
Holding sons whose hands curl about your thumb,
the grip it speaks of strength and those tomorrows
when footballs, baseballs, and basketballs
will occupy the hours.
I wonder how many passes have been thrown,
how many miles have been run?
They do it all so beautifully.
Was it yesterday when I held them
wondering about tomorrow?
Sleeping bundles in strange places,
how do they know that their parents
will take them home?

Worries ...
who has time to eat when play absorbs the day?
The first baseball game, he's only nine.
So we've waited these long years?
Nine plus nine and then some,
those dreams of sons and sports ...
they come and a pride swells ...
He's good! He's ours! It's done!
"Can I help, Dad?"
What is there to do, I'm almost done ...
"Sure son, here we're going to
(not a thought of I but we)
put this board here and then we'll
(again the two of us)
finish this job and play."
Ranches, houses, Lincoln Log adventures
on the floor ...
hours spent in building dreams,
sharing stories of the trail.
Then as ever,
home to Mom and the little ones.
Down the paths of the big chair,
the chest and coffee table,
we return exhausted from our feats.
A silent shadow sitting in the late afternoon sun
reading or retreating – both!
What dreams of hers
have formed the moments of the days?
Are they more or less what she expected?
I wonder?
Sons and daughters for fathers are a must.
They must be part of what she dreams,
so much of them is hers.

"Dad, one more shot ... PLEASE!"
"Okay son."
Pow!
"Dad! I got him!"
A running form of joy
seeks the treasure of the hunt.
Moments spent in life's long wait ... a triumph!
A special Colorado sky,
snow in August on the peaks,
the mirrored surface of a lake and fish.
"How big is he, Dad?"
"About six inches, son."
"I bet he weighs two pounds!"
For each and every one, these hopes and fears
I've carried now for years ...
through days of study
fraught with frustration,
wondering if I'd ever see my dreams come true;
to find a place with enough possibility
to give to each their due.
For them and me these days are spent
splashing in the pool,
a tennis match for all.
Can it finally be done?
A bulldozer is pushing down the trees ...
a light breaks across the land.
A sword that seeks the heart ...
a dream come true.
It will be done!
The earth is broken
and there rushes forth a fragrance
that seeps into the crevices of the soul.
Sustained for years
the dreams are still alive!

WANTING

Waxing in the portent always ends in waning.
I almost always see beauty as a dying thing
forcing faith to the forefront
as the only viable horizon.
Bobbing, browning grasses nod into Fall,
towards where the wind goes.
Why is my perception of beauty
lost in the hush after the wind?
Is each note, once played, gone forever?
My hope is to dance
– again –
for the last time.
The moon lies suffused in clouds,
white silver gleaming,
shrouding silent screams of fading life.
Roaring, thrusting jets
break the stillness of the night.
In their rumbling deaths
I seek, again,
the sanctuary of the stones.
Is there any time and place
where I can feel the One,
or will it be only in the rhythm of my running
and the exhaustion of my sleep?
Will I ever know the meaning of –
"Eternal rest grant unto them, Oh Lord,
and let perpetual light shine upon them."
Cries and orgasmic pulsating, cease in satiation.
Soft is the turn from dusk to dawn,
as the glowing pale moon
gives birth to a searing sun.

Ignorance finally fades to serenity.
I hear Him now,
"Focus on the open, free light
of conscious presence!"
The souls' eyes see the forthcoming –
"To live and die in service to becoming
– one with self –
a brother to my brothers and my sisters."
On the stage of
The Eternal,
as the crimson of the dawn and of the evening tide
become One,
I too,
seek to coincide
with the Eternal Flame.

DIASPORA

The coalescence of the All,
the light from the dark,
is the beginning of the birth of God.
As the universe breathes
so does the soul of God express itself.
We touch the face of the Effervescent
as we travel forward in time.

CAVE

Mist and rain, joy and pain,
time spent at the mouth of the cave.
Waiting.
Watching.
Wondering.
A natural reflective time,
a gift of the Process to us all.

HIM

I found Him in the Trilliums,
in the Jack in the Pulpits.
He was there in the ferns, lichens, and moss,
in the grasses.
There, in the Lady Slippers,
in the cones,
in the pitch,
in the swamps and hills.
An Omnipresence spoke in the light,
in the dark,
in the rain,
in the snow.
He touched my soul with His Heart,
wounded me with His Love.
Crystalline drops of blood drip
from some Eternal Source
filling a well from which all may drink.
His Voice said,
"Build a chapel in the forest.
Take stones and trees
and make a place of worship.
Invite those wandering by the wayside.
Create a banquet for strangers.
Walk with them in their trouble.
Listen to their hearts and minds.
Share in their journey.
Stand still in silence
beneath the mighty trees
and hold them.

There is more to this time than you know.
Do the faith that I require of you.
Do the hope that I ask of you.
Give of yourself,
that is all I require of you."
I heard His Voice in the evening.
I saw His Face in the sunsets.
I felt His Sword of Truth.
He opened my soul.
I dedicate this life to You.
The ground is ready.
The plans are done.
I will begin immediately.

PIECE OF WOOD

It died.
The giant old ponderosa,
finally, with roots loosened, strength spent,
could hold itself erect no longer.
The wind swept it down, far enough off the road,
not visible by passersby.
Yet I found it walking the fence line
on duty to my horses,
while mending disrespectful movement
of the elk.
There it was, roots upended, trunk laid down,
boughs left naked.
I made a mental note and several years later
went back to that spot,
severed trunk from roots and measured off several,
three to be exact,
eight-foot chunks.
I later split them lengthwise.
They made six benches for reflective repose,
four around the fire pits
and two next to the chapel in the garden,
rightful resting places for mighty wood.
Some several pieces of the branched old trunk
were put aside for firewood.
They waited,
until splitting exposed a heart of brilliant
soft red-yellow,
the many seasons of guarded sunlight.
Then, years later,
pulled from a stack late one winter's eve,
covered with ice crystals,
it was set upon the hearth in rack to wait.

Finally,
the evening's darkness and cold called it forth
to be placed on an open grate
and in that moment from memory's hall,
those days of Summer's labors
spent in work and fun
with my brother and his sons,
I did recall
as flames curling close began to extract
the sun's heat so generously stored.
The red-yellow heartwood reflected color
from the orange-white flames.
A perfect punctuation to the evening was made,
all in a piece of wood.

TO EMBODY

Point and counterpoint
the feminine and the masculine,
bodies with different strengths and purposes.
Complementary,
mysterious,
holding,
leading,
sharing,
never becoming one,
but growing side by side,
providing a laminate that produces
a greater strength.
The Truth is always something far greater
than we expect it to be,
or ever want it to be.
It is truly a Holy Grail that pulls us forward,
towards something far more omnipotent
than ourselves alone.
This pulling wrenches us at times
and haunts us at others.
It never leaves us quite alone.
Yet we are somehow brought into the realization
that some special union is at hand,
lover and beloved
upon a bosom of the Holy.
Not to stay!
The heart of God never stops beating.
Just to rest and then to spin off and away
in another journey that will lead us towards
self and circumstance.
A never ending dance, I move toward you and with you.
All of this now and forever.

HEAVEN SENT

What is this thing called life,
mundane delights,
or some holy universal purpose?
Lives bound by days and seasons.
And so ...
prayers are uttered in awe,
the anger long faded to
"True and doesn't matter."
The whisperings of the days and nights
all saying the same thing,
"He's here!"
The din, as the vortices interface,
becoming a Divine Orchestra
playing a symphony of perfection.
Its theme,
love melting into One.
Mystics and monks,
women saints,
dedications to purpose.
Hymns incessantly chanting,
"The joy of serving is all there is."
Touched by the Hand,
shocked into being,
alone with Him,
among the crowds,
in silence, seeing.
The mission:
Teaching others to see.
Forever holding mirrors,
reflecting souls' inner faces.
Standing ready,
listening for the next order.

A heart open to eternal logic that says,
"True, not true; mine, not mine."
One of the many witnesses
who bathe in a radiance of simple light.
All remembering an ancient prayer,
"As it was in the beginning is now
and ever shall be!"
I'm forever caught on
The Golden Staircase
in the eternal ecstasy of sharing One.

THE SUCKLING

A softer noise would be difficult to fathom,
at least in the human realm.
That gentle, wet, vacuuming
sound that says,
"Yes!"
Searching sustenance
with sentient delight.
A fertile slipping and sucking that begets
such satisfying murmurings –
from both!
A small little head nuzzling from side to side
groping for the liquid of life.
Urgent in its seeking,
yet contentment in its searching.
Ending,
finally with a sigh of being,
falling into itself.
A form cradled in that eternal pose,
an arm bent holding today's
and tomorrow's dreams.
And some still discuss the appropriateness
of nursing in public.

THE MILL

Only piles of twisted metal
sit in the early morning sun.
A caterpillar is busy pushing bits and pieces
into bunches to be recycled.
Nothing will remain!
The yard is empty.
Piles of mulch wait for lawns.
No rattling rigs encumbered with lumber,
no giant loader grabbing toothpicks
for the saw's teeth, no smell of sawdust
drifting through the neighborhood.
The sound of the whistle at noon is gone!
There is no call of "Timber!" from the loggers.
Only echoes of the sounds of their saws
from idle to flat out
chewing through branches and heartwood,
sending chilling memories through our minds.
No tinklings of the chains,
no caulked boots scraping bark,
or sending aloft a smoky powder
from some moss-hidden rock.
Jobs are lost.
A way of life is crushed.
No sweet scene of a wife and children
greeting a man smeared with black earth,
sawdust,
and sweat mixed with pitch.
The mystery man is gone who could
"take the big tree,"
and who knew when he touched it,
he stood in awe of its life.

There was more to it than a log and a dollar,
the feel of the bark,
the moss on the butt,
cobwebs and squirrels,
birds and porcupines.
No one gets closer to God's face
than a logger.
The children can't visit those mysterious spots
deep in the heart of the forest.
They can't watch their fathers
bringing sunlight to the ferns.
The snaps and crescendos of breaking branches,
and falling trees that spoke of man's presence,
now join the ranks of muffled history.
Only the pain of a semi-silence remains;
cruisers selecting some trees and leaving others,
that first dialog with the forest,
sawyers with their giant whirling saws
biting through history,
scalers seeking every inch of board from the logs.
Pullers and stackers making bundles of homes,
secretaries and accountants tracking profits from products,
marketeers sharing mountain slopes' gifts of warmth.
All were friends.
What will be missed?
For some – most of all the sight of
"the product" in their homes,
with the grain of the seasons sharing its grace
with us all.
When we are surrounded by insipid plastic
"grained if you will,"
there will be many things that will have been lost forever,
things we needed to feed our souls.

The environmentalists couldn't possibly understand.
How could they, they are too young.
For the most part they hike in synthetic boots
with their nylon knapsacks.
The politicos know much less.
And there were the legendary bureaucracies
with their fledglings
torn by their own economic needs
and an immature soul's cravings.
That's about all we had,
except the silent old ones
who could not quite articulate their arguments,
those who always knew enough
to leave some "old ones,"
"to keep alive the forests and the industry."
We didn't have time to learn to own the truths.
Was it the lack of planning,
too much planning,
multiple use,
sustained yield,
the spotted owl,
or was it the fact that we couldn't learn
to be honest fast enough
to adopt a posture that wouldn't
rape the forests and ourselves?
Grooming God's beard
is what we needed to learn to do.
The shavings would have continued
to feed our wonder forever.
Everything changes,
so they say ...
How long will I remember the day the mill died?
Let my prayer be *forever!*

THE PATH

Walk with measured confidence.
Is there beauty in the present?
Yes,
but there is also a veneer
and it is thin with too many lines,
not deep,
not of one substance,
not flowing from one to the next.
We need some eclectic breaks,
not too electric,
not too piecemeal,
but flowing organically.
We need some thread,
some touching,
some ability to be part of that
magnificent reality of history in the now.
When we get to the end of the row
in the vineyard,
we must look across the laden vines,
and remember:
In the end
life is always a personal choice.
It has always been a personal choice.
Self-coincidental movement,
not radical machinations,
or wild gesticulations.
It is not just a question of fiscal responsibility,
it is a matter of integrity.
We have now lost the integrity of the organic
and that is exactly what we need to rebirth.

In order to do that
we have to have the commitment
of enough of the people.
In my youth I was wind-swept
into the Holy Wars.
I witnessed the worst of men and the best of men.
I have sworn no allegiance to any ground,
or to any creed.
I worship with reverence the order of things:
the Truth of the Now.

TO ONE

Touching thighs,
soft to soft,
stomachs resting gently against each other.
Warmth,
melting into self,
a feeling of being one,
yet with another.
The centering coming from a quiet rest
belonging
only to One.
Knowing the self who can settle
into that still point,
to sense, feel, and see the other.
The miracle of silent presence,
giving my me to me and everything else.
A separate connectedness
that shouts into the abyss,
"I am!"

JUST LAVA

A little way off in the distance,
through trunks and strewn debris,
the ground made a gentle rise,
a swelling up of the earth.
I approach in wonder.
Lava had thrust up its jagged shoulders,
cracked, broken molten history,
all colonized by life.
Flat black and gentle gray faces,
catching sunlight
softened the hardness of the stone.
A huge twisted ponderosa stood on one side.
Curling roots hugging stone
held the pine.
Dens of porcupine, squirrels' pockets,
seeds scattered by birds
all made a show of their presence.
Then,
hanging in the shadows of the lee side,
ferns!
The mound, covered with moss and lichen,
still waits.
Brilliant and matted are the colors
of the altar's mantle of life,
orange, soft green, yellow and deep blue-gray
with hidden silver edges.
"Just an old rock,"
some say.

JUST ONE

Whether brass, string, drum, reed, or voice,
in height, depth, pitch, tone, sharp, or flat,
pain or joy is all one note.
Freedom to explore a range
in seeking self,
is all we are.
Standing alone,
reaching closer to the center,
adding our note to the forest's song,
choosing to become a part of
the eternal symphony of the wind,
a single note in His Score.
A thought comes:
Can I help another play their note,
hold their instrument,
guide the baton?
No –
Playing mine
is all that I can do.

LIGHT

Can I learn to see You better in darkness,
when Your golden light
is brightest at the edges?
In the brilliance of sunlit days,
with lids pressed shut to the brilliance
and warmth,
a pink-red softness
lights ways to the stillness of Your heart.
I see many wavering lustrous paths –
Which is mine?
I hunger for Your touch,
Your scent, Your presence.
In the storms of summer,
when thunder shudders through my body,
I sit again with eyes closed and seek
to capture Your essence –
You come!
Why is it that I hear Your footsteps so clearly
in the breezes of the day,
when closed to the light I wait?
And in the cold of the blizzard,
eyes slit to the wind,
the razor's edges of Your crystals
touch my face.
Your deserts dance with moonlight
as blue-black shadowed rivulets run towards
Your feet.
Tracks upon the sand lead me to Your House.
Finally, in Your arms,
I rest when blackness creeps in
from all directions.

FROM THE MOUTH OF THE CAVE

From mouths of caves
we stand gawking at the end of the day
into the setting sun,
our faces agape in ignorance and awe.
The hours spent burning,
burning the mountains of Chapas,
on the planes of the Serengeti,
through the jungle of the Amazon,
across the Nordic reaches.
Flames consume a piece of every continent,
save that mysterious frozen expanse
beyond the southern horizon.
And so ...
we also dumped untold tons of gallons
of poisons in the rivulets,
streams, rivers, lakes, and oceans.
Then too,
we belched toxins into the air
of myriad pristine valleys.
Frenetic in our death pace we rush back and forth,
up and down,
across and through, over and under
our streets and avenues,
forests and plains, Chainman shale and mountains,
the seas and stars.
Who would die if we all stood still?
Dumbfounded,
we stand and watch life drip
into the deserts of time.

WORSHIP

A god?
A church?
A congregation?
A vast and wondrous vista?
I stand in awe
through so many encounters.
Senses reel,
a presence I'm sure.
Just mine in the fleeting vortices of physics?
Hardly!
I see You and I see so much.
Thank you!

ME

I am cursed with myself!
"Do it!"
What?
"Build a chapel, an altar and pews!
Write the stories!
The Rules
and the poetry!"
How?
"Little by little!
Design it!
One plan!
Lay the groundwork!
One building!
Pour the footing!
One word at a time!
One book!
One poem!
Redesign!
Redesign!
Rewrite!
Rewrite!
And
Rewrite!"
* * *
Fatigue and time,
the incessant rush of the parts dulls the edge.
Finally! The silence sharpens the blade
and the Sword of Truth cuts to the quick.
"Do myself NOW!
That's all!"
I am cursed and blessed with myself!

YOUR WHISPER

In silence so profound,
I know You do abound.
Because as a thought comes and startles me,
I take sail on life's great eternal sea.

SNOWFLAKE I

From how high up,
how far over
did your journey begin?
I see you wind-whipped and dashing,
now gently floating,
drifting slantingly across the meadow.
I watch as you add your gift
to the indistinct white mantle,
only to be discovered again
in the moon's garden of diamonds.
Then finally,
nestling next to fellow flakes
your star-like arms and legs touch and mingle
with your brothers and your sisters.
I see you all waiting now
to become that transparent drop,
a brilliant, reflective, shimmering transformation,
forming a bridge
from solid to liquid to life.

SNOWFLAKE II

Cascades of white come.
Forms of fixed sharp crystal's oneness
are touched by warmth.
Converging in letting go,
sagging to gray,
transpiring as sun rays regather their brilliance,
the coalescence slips into transparent rivulets.
Vanishing,
you leave dusty trails
on my skylight.

A BREATH

Taken while sobbing,
rasping with death,
imperceptible in fear.
Deeply drawn,
shallow,
hesitatingly,
panting.
All part of our
yin and yang.
With it
we draw truth
across palates
and
from palettes.

A CONVERSATION

And the young man said as he walked away,
"I'm going off to explore the world,
to learn about things and people."
The soft firm voice of the old man said,
"I'll wait here for you."
The youth strode away into the sunset.
The old man sat and carved his burled wood,
splitting pieces off to get something
"about" the right size and shape.
Then he slowly sanded each piece to fit.
Meanwhile, the youngster was off and about
looking for the right sizes and shapes
of things and of people
and asking many questions.
He got few answers
and grew bored with his exploration.
Soon he began to ride to
"cover more ground and to learn more."
After some time
he wondered what the old man was doing
and grew lonesome
and returned from his travels.
The old man asked,
"What did you learn?"
The young man thought,
"Why didn't he ask what I had seen?"
The old man mused,
"Wood is like people,
if you treat it gently, over time
it performs its tasks very well."

The young man sat and watched
as the old carver started
with something that was close
and brought it slowly to close enough.
Looking at the pleasant countenance
of the old man
he said,
"All things take time to learn to do well,
don't they?"
"Yes, they do,"
the old man murmured.
"Perfection is an illusion, isn't it?"
the young man offered.
A gentle nod of the old bearded head
was his reply.
The youngster added,
"How much is too little
and how much is too much
is what we all have to learn, isn't it?"
Smiling and placing a gnarled, loving hand
on the young man's shoulder, he said,
"Now you are beginning to play
The Game of Life!"

A GLANCE

I look upon the meadow
and see waving grass
bowing in gentle undulations,
saying always
"Yes!" to time.

ALMOST ...

In grief we fight from moment to moment,
never knowing
yesterday's truths or tomorrow's lies.
With blinders on we see only cataracts of time,
falling, falling,
dropping off to God knows where.
I seek to know,
help me in my unknowing.
And finally,
When shall I know that the intellect knows so little?
When from the depths of some abyss
pristine drops of water come,
and touching me
they find and baptize a soul
wanting, wanting
so much to be touched by the truth,
to be free.
How could I know how wonderful it feels
to be self if it were not for you?
And what do I say
when the gentle breeze calls for a response?
Madness is just madness.
Glory lies to justify the madness.
And yet,
in their souls lies a hidden time
when truth is one.

AS IF ...

It's almost as if I stood on the edge of a savannah,
the mouth of a cave,
the end of a pier,
at a drawbridge,
waiting.
Expectations,
what were they?
In their eyes
an outcast,
in truth, a missionary.
Where is that road to that serene Nordic shore?
How long before we rest?
How long before we are free,
lying with the softness of the sun,
walking in the gentle mist?
And where is the breeze,
with the crispness of the air
full of birds
following the winds of Spring,
northward,
"Seeking fuller being,
bringing closer union?"

BEFORE AND AFTER

Soft:

A curling presence,
contours of rolling hills, gullies,
fountains, crevasses and caverns,
warmth harboring passions.

Hard:

A human plane,
broad back,
flat to touch,
emanating heat source
– letting go.

THE BRASS RING

The sights and sounds
all mixed with color and movement
as pressing bodies moved along the Midway.
Then I saw it,
the carousel with its calliope
matching the muffled whirring of its engine,
dancing, golden-colored horses, and ...
and the brass ring.
Some barker may have said,
or my parents might have explained,
to catch the brass ring
"was to be special."
It was to ride the horses free.
Could I ride?
Can I try?
Smiling faces must have let me.
Was I lifted or did I mount myself?
'Round and 'round we went
closing in on the goal.
Could I reach it?
I can try!
No, not quite!
Up and down and around again
stretching farther this time.
I hear the voices and see the faces
of parents and relatives.
Then, it's mine!
I wanted it!
I stretched out for it and I got it!
Just a brass ring, some would say,
a small prize for a little boy.

Not so!
The efforts and the dream
set mighty sails in a young man's heart.
With them he charted great oceans,
scaled grand peaks.
The seed of
I can!
bore fruit in every endeavor.
To think you can and want to try
– then to be given a hopeful chance by parents –
gives fertile ground to youthful spirits
and sets desire in young hearts.

CABIN LOGS

Charred lifeless spires
left in fire's wake,
branches stiff and broken,
needles nothing but drifting ashes,
wind scattered on the forest floor.
The size is right and the bark is tight,
beetles have yet to find their delight.
For me you are sought after, "cabin logs"
that are Oh just so right!
You drop with a deadly thud.
Nothing stops you except burned brown earth.
Your swaying's all dead now.
The axe slices your sides
and beneath I behold the mottled cambium,
yellow gold to umber and white.
Drawn knife peels your skin
leaving tracks of shallow dishes in your grain.
Knots are black-silver eyes
jutting from your flanks
just before they are shaved close,
leaving shiny hearts of ringed life.
My mind says,
"Which to kitchen, bath and bedroom?"
The burly ones with brutish knobbiness
laden with character
are, of course,
for the reflective chapel cells.
Did I know when watching boiling, rising smoke
that I would be blessed
to capture such sweetness
in bringing logs to resting places?

CHILDREN

Conjugal love
Labor's pain
Soft bundle
Relief
She and rascal – fine
Demands
Hours
Fatigue
Ecstasy
Pride
Disappointments
Lessons
Deeds
Broken moments
Anger flares
Compassion's repose
Future's dreams
Yesterday's mount
Endless hopes
In them
Through them
By them

* * *

Sacred sounds increasing humanity
Following Greek wisdom,
"Better to be than not to be ..."
We populate the land
Giving life to others
Sharing, being
Slow enough to give them learnings of our kind
Respectful always of history's deep commitment
For us, them, theirs

FALL

Are snowflakes now falling,
and are the ducks and geese still calling?
Tell me!
Is Fall thresholding through the jagged,
naked twigs
that seek to catch and hold that rising, burning disk
that sets coyotes' voices to the wind
and owls to their haunting hooting?
Have the does recovered
from their burdens of Spring,
and are they gray and sleek with small shadows
standing gently at their sides?
Are there silver caps on the shore's stones
where waves have left themselves
congealed in crystal castles?
Is there a crispness in the wind carrying a chill,
sending shivers and giving a thrill?
Does that pungent smell of a shotgun hang
to mix with feathers felt through cold fingers
retrieving pheasants from their fall?
Are silent seconds spent in searching skies
split with "cawluks" as rowing ravens
rend the air?
Have the round, yellow, heavy heads of the goldenrod drooped
and are they now wearing white hair
with gray beards,
having had their pollen pulled from stamens
and pushed into pregnant places?
Is the earth's heavy breathing through the night
left on brown, broken stems in the morning's
early light?

Are roaring, whining chainsaws sending
savage teeth
through aspens strung like jack sticks
sheltered in the ferns?
Are pairs of water skis resting relics in their racks
waiting to be stored?
Are Summer's traveled trails tracked
with coon, mink and fox
moving from puddles on to ponds,
then to bait and box?
Has pole-wood been whacked to lengths
and stacked with golden circles
sharing stories
of each Winter and its Spring?

HEY MOM! HEY DAD!

Free from encumbrances
the mind moves gently back in time
to recapture those lost moments
when the sun's rays and the warmth were all that was.
You will never know – so I will tell you ...
How many times I remember Grampa's farm,
the stillness and the all-encompassing warmth,
the security,
the sense of permanence.
And the food was Oh so good!
Was it because it was made with love
or was it that the appetite gained from
the day's activities was so great,
or both?
I remember a sunny afternoon herding huge cows
when one turned and suddenly came at me.
I made a mad dash for the fence.
I think it took me several years
to get over the feeling of fright
from that giant beast.

* * *

I have lived at the crest of the wave,
at the tip of the branch,
on the leading edge of the wind,
a precipice always immediately there before me.
The arduous and tortuous circumstances
have given me moments of exultation
and moments of desperation.
There is now a need for meditation
and the softer time to reflect and recreate –
to store that strength for the next encounter.

SELF PORTRAIT

Dear children, this is me.
What price a man?
Who is that truck driver who walks
slowly to his rig,
bag in hand, destination lying ahead,
alone on the road.
Who is that old man?

* * *

Who was that little boy
who would carve a crucifix on a tree?
That was me.
Who was that little boy
who felt so lonesome when he was growing up?
That too, was me.
Who was that dreamer
who dreamt strange dreams?
It was me.
Who was that little boy who needed love so much?
Yes, that was me.
Who cried with his dog
and wondered about life?
Yes, that was also me.
Who hunted alone
and talked to his God?
That too, was me.
Who took the candy bar from the store
and returned it?
Yes, it was me.
Who loved to play on the team
and give it his best?
It was me.

Who wouldn't eat strange foods
no matter what the price?
That was me.
Who stood and looked at the marsh
and felt the call of the loon?
That too was me.
Who cried crystal tears
as dreams were put on hold?
Yes, it was me.
Who thought often of children and home
when he was far away and alone?
Yes, that was me.
Who wanted to be there
gently stroking flowing hair?
That too, was me.
Who sang Christmas carols in June
and laughed at the moon?
It was me.

QUESTIONS

But Dad, why do you pursue your dream?
Why am I doing it?
In a five-month season with twelve cabins,
each with four people, for twenty years –
and that is just my turn ...
That is approximately 144,000 sunsets
and 36,000 moonrises.
There will be untold laughing and crying,
moments of love unfolding.
And that doesn't even count the birds and the bees
that will enjoy our flowers.
And you ask,
Why do you do it, Dad?

CITIES

Cities, I wonder what they're for?
Do we know?
The Greeks had a moment in time
that produced magnificence
and a reflection of the human process.
We too,
are productive in our own way.
Is this the way
we generate the best for the species?
When we congeal into masses
we see the totality of
the results of our communal efforts,
good and bad.

A DISTANT DREAM

I see in a distant dream ...
An alpine meadow in the green.
I see in a distant dream ...
You standing amidst the mist and steam.
I see in a distant dream ...
A child's fresh face pressed to Spring's window screen.
I see in a distant dream ...
Your hair touched by a golden beam.
I see in a distant dream ...
A young man's mind beginning to glean.
I see in a distant dream ...
A bridal gown fitting at the seam.
I see in a distant dream ...
Tears caused that I did not mean.
I see in a distant dream ...
Peanuts, liqueur and cream.
I see in a distant dream ...
A family that age begins to wean.
I see in a distant dream ...
A daughter's heightened high school preen.
I see in a distant dream ...
A Christmas with people, pie and ice cream.
I see in a distant dream ...
Sons and dogs growing tall and clean.
I see in a distant dream ...
My Angel caught in a silent scream.
I see in a distant dream ...
A father's family going lean.
I see in a distant dream ...
Snow, sleigh and a silver team.

I see in a distant dream...
Tasha bathing in the moon's shimmering sheen.
I see in a distant dream...
Life as an emptying stream.
I see in a distant dream...
The end of life I mean.
I see in a distant dream...
A crystal staircase gleam.
I see in a distant dream...
Two children playing in eternal ween.

THOUGHTS IN A HOTEL ROOM

Square rooms, square doors,
form dictates content.
I am who I am,
condemned to be all me.
My history,
my now,
leads me to the tasks at hand.
I can only do that in which I believe.
There are no extraneous exercises.
Each act leads me to myself.

INVASIONS

Pock-marked intrusions
in the blackness of the night.
Why does man insist on marking his presence
with an artificial light,
to better make his way in the twilight or the dawn,
or to ward off his neighbors
from whom all trust is gone?

* * *

When the sun goes down and I turn
to the quitting of the day,
among my many thoughts
a good night to my God I say.
I do not want a mercury vapor light
hanging someplace overhead,
sharing its artificial glow,
invading dusky moments in my bed.
With its eerie green light
it casts a different hue.
Where are all those fading forms that used to mix
with the evening's fading blue?
With eyes offended
and adjusting to the artificial light,
I seek to see and understand
throughout the long and lonely night.
Finally,
a tiny crescent rises in heaven's hallowed hand,
sharing its golden-silver satin
with the greenness of the land.
In the misty droplets of the dawn
how secret still is the moon's soft glow,
as I bustle through the 21st century
wondering who it is that is my foe?

LIFE GIVEN

I passed a moment there, back then
that made me wonder if and when
there ever is a chance to feel
what a mother, son, or daughter seal
in moments spent just sitting in the sun?
Morning stints with jobs all done
and afternoons with thoughts of darkness
ending tenderly with a gentle kiss.
Do these moments of repose
taken quickly, always close
that gap that comes when birth is given,
or the course in daylight driven?
Somehow I think there is a time
in those moments of life's prime
when a woman sits with chin in hand,
thoughts gently sifting through the sand,
cementing cells forever in a lasting bond of love
as time's strings are pulled gently from above.
Can a father learn to enjoy a girl or a boy
and all that goes with the giving of a toy,
if often in those early years
his presence causes only tears?
Take the necessary steps to be
in a way that's easy for all to see,
you too understand how the gift of life is won.
Stay to share those fleeting moments in the sun.

MAN

Oh man, why does the quest congest?
Does this give heat to cement the elements
to produce a fine crystal, that when struck
issues forth a sweet symphony of even frequencies?
Or,
are we ignorant of the process
and invent as we progress?
Stumbling over flowers
placed to provide organic sustenance,
bumping into self and others,
we scurry to our graves.

PETRO

Pumps peck the land
like huge birds rising on their haunches,
dipping their beaks,
gorging their voracious appetites
on black nectar of forgotten fossils.
A pungent odor
permeates the privileged place ...
Oil country!

FOR REEFUS –
MOMENTS IN THE LIFE OF A FISH AND A BOY

The huge snout of the big old trout
wriggled all about as he poked in and out.
Having feasted his full
and being burdened with gout,
he certainly knew what life was about.
Swinging his mighty angular head
he slowly swam around his bed
admiring his color, a bright and stately red.
It occurred to him it had been some time
since he had fed.
He moved in his stream as if it were cream,
his mind ablaze with a delightful dream
of a new mayfly all pretty and clean.
One he could own and then bask in his preen.
He was old and bold, and his story told
he'd lived in the stream through the heat
and the cold.
His confidence was legendary,
there wasn't a fisherman he could be sold.
Rising to the surface, he broke it with a slam,
grabbing fly after fly he began to cram
his big old mouth like he was eating Spam.
Mighty conqueror of his dominion,
back and forth he swam.
As far as he knew there were only a few
who ate as he did and grew and grew
in the icy waters of the river so blue.
Fellow trout shied away from him, it was true.
After taking his meal he moved off to steal
a nap, so later he could feel alive, ready and real.

Then, moving through the shallows,
his back breaking the surface like a keel,
he went to his hole, knowing he would never be
the victim of a fly fisherman's reel.
Alone, he stayed away from the crowd,
he hated their noise and thought they were loud.
Swishing his tail he settled under a cloud,
resting and snoozing and feeling very proud.
Suddenly a movement caught his eye,
something strange hit the water
as it fell from the sky.
He blinked and looked and wondered why
and then another katydid to the surface did fly.
There was a flash off to the left of his old hole
and he froze and looked to see if it was a rod or a pole.
Weaving and moving along the bank from nearby knoll,
was it the wind, a fisherman, or a red-headed troll?
He was sure it was not the right season,
a katydid? It was all without reason.
The thought, however,
to the old trout was pleasin'.
He looked and he thought it just could be treason.
No trout would ever gain a respectable size
unless he lived and learned until he was wise,
all there was to know about the various flies,
because indeed, those fishermen
were intelligent guys.
The afternoon was spent hour after hour
watching a veritable zoo land with such power.
They would swat the water making a huge shower,
cast down from above as though thrown from a tower.
Then it happened, it came at just the right angle,
alighting gently and moving, showing a spangle.

There was no adjacent unnecessary jangle,
a delicious tidbit with which he could tangle.
He couldn't stand the sight
of the may nymph in flight.
With a quick stroke he struck
with all of his might.
He was so sure, it looked so right.

* * *

The day was late and almost past,
the little boy's arm was tired to the last.
It moved so slowly he could hardly cast
the only fly in his box, a nymph,
didn't move very fast.
The little boy truly loved to fish,
a trip with his father was his only wish.
He was seven, a redhead and somewhat tallish
and the zest with which he fished
was matched by his refusal of the dish.
For years there wasn't a time
when upon entering a sporting goods store,
if he had a dime,
that he wouldn't argue with his father
how each fly was prime,
achieving at moments a description sublime.
During evening talks about the stars
when questions were raised
about Venus and Mars,
he would saturate the conversation with ises and ares
about astral streams and rivers chock-full of gars.
He was really a swell little guy
who hated nuts and loved apple pie.
He was totally honest and never told a lie,
except maybe when he spoke of a trout and a fly.

The trip had been planned,
the stream selected as the best in the land.
The food all bought, the clothes all packed,
it was to be grand.
He was so excited to hold a trout in his hand.
The alarm clock was set so early they could rise,
when stars were the only things to be seen in the skies.
He went to the closet and up on his chair
to reach for his flies
and in the process he knocked to the floor
all of his father's ties.
The flies all packed, their beds all made,
they were off with their dreams of pools and shade.
Their goodbyes all bade,
the trip was made
at last to the stream and the glade.
The journey was long and took quite awhile.
The little guy sat thinking of trout with a smile.
He was so sure and confident of his swimming-pool style,
afternoons had been spent in casting flies
and developing guile.
After some hours the little boy began
to nod and doze,
his tiny freckled, sunburned nose
bobbing like a tattered rose
striking a perfect Rockwell pose.
They finally arrived, the man and the boy.
He rushed to the stream and returned full of joy.
Grabbing his rod and flies he was off with his toy,
knowing those trout couldn't resist his ploy.
The long day was spent casting,
switching flies that were lent
from father to son.

His tiny arms were weak and rent
and with a wistful look he glanced at the tent.
Not even one little trout
had seen fit to give the tiny sprout
a nibble as he sent fly after fly to the water,
in and out.
He was beginning to weaken
and even to doubt.
The sun was setting on the balsams in the west
as the little boy threw the small fly to his guest.
He was determined to give this old hole
one last test,
then off to the tent, a fire and a night full of rest.
The tiny nymph rose from the tip of his rod,
circling in the air in a manner quite odd.
The boy with a prayer sent off to his God
set the fly gently to the surface to plod.

* * *

The nymph vanished from sight
in a swirl of water and light.
The drooping line snapping tight,
zipping through the water as dark as night.
Jerking his rod and setting the hook, he turned to his father
only to see him reading a book.
He shouted, "Hey Dad! I got one that took!"
His father jumped up and ran over to look.
The little boy's expression was all in his eyes.
They were wide with wonder and full of surprise.
He had imagined a trout taking one of his flies,
but never one of such enormous size.
The hook had been set as the trout took to flight,
the little boy gripped the rod with both hands
so tight.

As the huge fish felt the pull of the line
he knew he must fight
as the sun stopped at the tree tops
to lend its last light.
The old fish turned as he jumped and crashed,
moving in and out of the shallows his huge body flashed.
The line remained taut as through the water he slashed,
then rising again to the surface
he smashed.
The little boy's mind was all in a daze,
this would be one of his most memorable days.
He wondered if he would ever be able to raise
the big fish from the dark water's shifting haze.
Through the twilight the two sought to do battle.
From the boy with the fish came no idle prattle.
Standing on the bank his feet slipped to rattle,
then finally exhausted, he sat in a spraddle.
His feet were all wet
when he called for the net.
Then he whispered, "He's a whopper I bet,
but I know I'm going to get him yet."
Finally the huge fish surfaced and rolled.
His life was ending, his soul was bold.
But now it was over, the story full told.
The little boy had beaten him sure as gold.
The father watched the boy as he reeled him in
and the huge fish's back showed dark and thin.
When he neared the shallows,
he was too tired to spin
and the young man at last broke into a grin.
A son with his dad standing silently in the sand
watched the net slide beneath the great fish
and finally placed in his hand.

Slowly they stepped together
from shore to the land,
their arms encircled in a loving band.
That night after he ate he listened to his father tell
how he had watched with pride
as his heart did swell.
And just after that, to sleep exhausted he fell
as the silence of the forest said its farewell.
They returned home the very next day
and for a while the little boy
didn't have much to say.
He wasn't even interested in going out to play.
His mother wondered about the trip,
the fish and the stay.

* * *

Hanging there on the study wall
eyes twinkling, he remembered that Fall
and watched as the years turned the boy
to a man, very tall.
The old fish just smiled at the redhead
and knew it all.
Sometimes the young man
would stand and gaze
at the big old trout who'd hung there
all those many days.
As a path through memories would blaze,
slowly a tear would silently raise
and gently tumble down faded freckles.

THE WIND

The wind,
tossing, turning, twisting,
soft, stirring, smashing,
buffeting, billowing, bellowing, blasting,
calm, churning, crashing,
pausing, pushing, puffing,
chilling, carrying, causing,
is the breathing of the world.
To touch the wind
is to sense the soul of the earth.

A SYMPHONY

From the soup of smog
strings of an orchestra break forth
signaling at least enough are present
to give support to the soul.
But because of the congestion
is the music soothing,
restful, and creative?
And does this give us pause to reflect
on the sufficiency of society?
Few – some – many – a lot – too many –
enough.
Where is the health of the species today?
Is it in the cities of the globe?
There must be some,
I hear the symphony.
Yet I think we have moved
from wandering tribes to condensed urban centers
in too short a time.
A person needs to live alone with others
to progress to an ownership of the self,
then,
along with others,
shape a shared integrated environ
that hosts the youth
and favors creative responsibility
and fundamental integrity.
I muse,
the symphony has yet to miss a note.
Is it already here?

TECHNOLOGY

As I walked out of the television studio,
having delivered a piece
on the unmanageableness of media
and its problematic role in the world,
I looked up at the 30-foot satellite dish
next to the station.
Nestled gently
against the bottom of the disk
and a support strut,
was a bird's nest ...
a most beneficial use of modern technology.

TIRED PARENT

Who is at the door?
Is it a kid, or a person?

WHO ARE THEY?

As wind parts
blowing hair held up by bandanas and headbands,
the young couple on a motorcycle
move into their future.
Faded jeans and tennis shoes –
(socks, who wears them anymore?)
flash by.
The tote bag says,
"Drink Water!
It's the Real Thing!"
Who are they?
Where are they going?
What will they do with their lives?

DRAGONS

There is a manifold season of Dragons out there.
Must I continue to read The Psalms?
Is contrite supplication my only alternative?
The never-ending bridge to self is long indeed.

* * *

There is only to sit the Charger
and meet the dawn with sword in hand.

THE SWAMP
JUST SOUTH OF THE HOUSE

I remember the first time I ever heard/saw
that magnificent mysterious spot.
My father took me one evening –
long before the house was built on the hill.
We were "picnicking" at the Quonset.
Frogs were singing,
and to satisfy a child's curiosity,
he took me there.
In the darkness of the evening
there was a sense of awe and some fear –
he must have held my hand.
I remember crescendos of frogs
and the stillness of the water
as it lay like pieces of broken silver-black mirrors
between clumps of brown and bent grasses
hanging over little pools,
hiding
(I'm still absolutely sure)
something very valuable.
There were also bunches of tag alder
and crisscrossed rotting logs
with their flattened and well-worn muskrat paths,
barely visible in the darkness
of the late evening light,
looking like little secret trails
leading off to some humble, safe place.
The incredible symphony
along with the soft stillness of the reflection
of the gold of the moon
and the white silver of the stars
in the openings between the dark shadows
on the water, left an imprint

that was never to be forgotten
and never to be quite understood.
(Paths leading to the soft, Sacred Peace
of God's Hand are never fully owned.)
Time passed and a child grew,
and visited the swamp in the daylight.
The challenges then were of "action,"
the exuberance of youth,
jumping from clump to clump,
avoiding the "boiling black oil"
of the "Mean One."
Yes,
there were brief seconds
when I stopped to SEE the small piles
of dissipating marsh grasses
that had formed the muskrats' home,
and wondered if there might not be
something more to it all.
But then,
as with all living things,
I succumbed to the push of youth and time
and took myself across the swamp
to "the other side"
and it was done!
Conquered and forgotten –
almost.
Years passed and the swamp dried up
and disappeared.
I grew up and went on about
my conquest of thought,
word and deed.

Then,
one day I was asked what I thought about
and I remembered the swamp.
I realized that there was some unfinished business
that needed taking care of –
a "Thank You" to my father for taking me there
and the expression of a deep gratitude
for the awe that struck
the soul of a small boy
that lived in some hollow of his heart
and never died.
There is a knowledge and a gratefulness
of a gentle, soft time
when I was given an opportunity
to look into the Eyes of God.
Now,
as I hunt for a piece of land some sixty years later,
I realize all I ever wanted to do
was to take a piece of ground
and turn it into a retreat
for others to see into God's Eyes.
I still labor at the task.

MONARCHS

Streams of butterflies drop
from billowing gray-blue skies
flutter about
finally perch
on tattered leaves
of late October branches.
While
caribou range Denali,
wolves play,
porcupines waddle
from browse to waiting browse.
Windows glow
laden with vistas
of eternity.

Streams of butterflies drop
from billowing gray-blue skies
flutter about
finally perch
on tattered leaves
of late October branches.
While
here–there
candles flicker in Buddhist monasteries.
Strobe lights strike dance-floor patterns.
Owls break late afternoon silence.
Insistent breezes buffet lacy boughs.
Sunrays pierce
sagging rainforests.

Streams of butterflies drop
from billowing gray-blue skies
flutter about
finally perch
on tattered leaves
of late October branches.
While
lowing herds shuffle
from meadows to barns.
Whiskered cats lick rivulets from pails.
Mice scamper from grain to burrow.
Bombs explode.
(On purpose and otherwise.)
Life ripped from caring souls.

Streams of butterflies drop
from billowing gray-blue skies
flutter about
finally perch
on tattered leaves
of late October branches.
While
children laugh and play.
Snow drifts rest.
Rivers swell,
run to seas.
A bell ends trading
on Wall Street.
Heaped garbage reeks.

Streams of butterflies drop
from billowing gray-blue skies
flutter about
finally perch
on tattered leaves
of late October branches.
Do the mission!
Then what?
Spinning crowds weave trails.
Leaves feed humused carpets.
Dark descends
while
I stand
amidst clouds
of Monarchs
settling
at Rancho Aguililla,
resting
from their journey
to their purpose.

MY LAST WONDER

Has my presence
helped to cause another
to say, "Yes!"?

JUAN DE ARAGON

Found in archives of the Pyrenees, Egypt, Arabia, Persia,
India, Judea and at the Iron Gates
were pieces that led me to myself.
The question was always:
From whence comes the travails
of the Pilgrims of the ages?
Down what well-trodden paths
have the discalced and calced
wandered before orders were established,
caves abandoned,
and lepers haunted hidden trails?

* * *

Unrecorded histories of the multitudes
swirl and mix
with rare, forgotten, and never-known saints
whose trust in truth
banished the malevolence and ignorance
roiling from the vagabond minds of barbarians
while bridges to the present
were constructed and destroyed.
Civilization's mesmerizing dance,
two steps forward, one step, or two, backward
created a shuffle of yeses and nos
bewildering the wise
and obfuscating the enlightened.
It was a time when coins of copper, silver, and of gold
foretold the future of the seas,
and births and deaths of nations yet unborn.
All this while the People,
on the bridge to more than, better than,
looked to the future for perfection.
Hiding from their hour,
the past and present,
where always their choices
were laden with eternal gifts.

Lives were squandered under shackles
of tribal chieftains,
while scribes recorded and recorded
the archives guarded and torched.

* * *

As the lexicon of Latin
larded its hold on the throats of most,
a literati, a monk of late vocation,
wandered barren and cobbled highways
and byways
from monastery to monastery
searching for the word of God.
Yes,
he had read the parchments of the ancients.
Yes,
he spoke eight languages,
and at 50 had not yet written his first word.
His mind was full of prayers,
some from others' mutterings,
most from his own sentiments.
They were breathed into damp evenings
and misty mornings from vale
or from mountain top,
always giving Alabanzas to the Holy One.
A *"thank you"* was forever
his most profound utterance.
From a precursor, the Francis who had come,
for all those Francises yet to come.
Those who always came
from the cataclysms of their times,
who, when touched by the mystery of forgiveness,
stretched their understanding
and embraced the All.
Brother or sister, race or creed, plant or animal,
differences blending to magnificent incidentals.

All majestic beauty
vibrating in the rustling of the Divine's
flowing robes,
and thus,
deserving of the admonition:
Treat everything with
knowledge, care, responsibility, and respect.
Bowing his head he prayed a deeper and deeper
"Thank you!"
to the All of the unknowns and knowns.
And so it was on that fateful day,
standing on the path overlooking Lucerne,
he vowed to find words of God.
Those simple words of the vernacular
bathing the soul with crystalline tears
and sending one into raptures
lost in the radiance of the wake
of the Divine's reverberating light.
"To see or to perish"
always on his lips.
Dropping to his knees he said,
"One word with which to hold."
And as if moved by the strength
of his conviction,
he picked up a twig and wrote his first word,
"Yes!"
Startled by the profundity of his actions
and the presumption of his purpose,
he gathered the dust of his word and cast it into the air
as the sun's first rays flooded the path
and, sparkling with a brilliance,
illuminated the entire countryside.
In that ecstasy of grasping his three letters
from the earth
and witnessing the dance of light radiating
from horizon to horizon, he said,
"I will search the archives for Your words.

I will lay them at Your feet.
I will set them down for all to see
and in a manner which they can understand."
With renewed vigor he rose from his knees
and began searching
from parchment to parchment.
Which word would open the door to Truth?
What word would provide a stone on which to stand,
a still point giving anyone their
"Yes!"?
So he sought those stones
as he spent his days wandering
through the monasteries of his world,
seeking those linking words from warring cultures.
Utterances that touched the souls of men,
made them stop dead still
upon the battle fields of their times,
where dropping to their knees they breathed
"Yeses!"
which took them from those beastly clashes
to meadows and hearths where love is born
and births bring forth rushing seeds of hope
sown in the pockets of souls
that would forever sing
praises to the Divine.

* * *

And so,
Juan de Aragon,
lost in wanderings
amidst tome-stacked, darkened archives
came upon his first find.
Three glorious years of fruitless searchings
baptized his journey with hours spent
traversing far and wide,
finding and reading the sheltered
wisdom of the ages.

Hills and paths beyond number,
monasteries, both large and small,
targets of his seeking will.
Knowledge thus gained
had opened heart and mind
to the tenacity of human spirit
and the malevolence of the baseness of lost souls.
Eyes, burdened with seekings
and the flickerings of candles,
saw the first stone,
a rock-word upon which he would build
a temple to his God.
It was found in the Pyrenees.
Flashing before him,
grounding him again to his dedicated purpose,
his heart leaped for joy
as eyes closed in silent prayer.
Rushing through aisles of ancient parchments,
he reached a bench and desk.
Quickly,
taking stylus in hand with trembling anticipation,
he dipped in the well a tool
that he had only seen Others use.
The many Others of dedication,
those who would capture history's ruminations
for yet Others who would come and decipher,
or guess at significances that another time
would attribute to their markings.
Reaching to the shelf above
and gently extracting a small scroll of clean parchment,
knowing his words would not be many,
only a few and simple,
causing stirrings in the body
and quickenings in the soul,
making those who came across them
tremble with the same excitement he felt
when he discovered them.

Slowly he penned his first word,
"Umzo!"
That is to say,
"Be One!" Or Play One!
as it is now understood.
"Yes!"
he breathed into the dark, silent recesses
of the ancient archive.
"I begin a new life and upon these stone-words
I will construct Your Temple.
To you,
The One,
this first stone-word will form the foundation
upon which everything will lie."
Reverently,
he rolled the scroll into a tight bundle,
secured it with a sheepskin thong,
and tucked it deep within his tunic.
Exiting the confines of the monastery,
having thanked his brothers for their generosity,
his eyes were lifted to cloud-decked skies
and streams of golden staircases
reaching to the heavens.
Upon them Juan sent prayers to his God,
to the angels and their minions.
His days were filled with joy
as weeks and months were filled with wanderings.
Thus years were spent in hope and prayer
as sight dimmed and legs bowed
to time spent upon the trails.

* * *

The second was found in Egypt,
hidden and forgotten in a small monastery
among the hills along the Nile.
Having finished exhausting days
while reading the last of the scrolls,
a stillness rippled through his body
and a silence covered his ears
as his eyes closed upon the last word
of the scroll.
It leapt from the parchment
in a flash of warmth and consuming brilliance.
All consternation and fatigue vanished
and a peace of such depth held his soul
as he whispered another
"Yes!"
Holding silence in respect of truth encountered,
he slowly moved to the adjacent desk and bench.
Lifting the stylus for the second time
he wrote
"Napan!"
Be Still!
A glorious, sacred simplicity
smothered all sound,
leaving only a depth of One sharing one.
Praising good fortune,
he took his tired body to meal with his brothers.
Raising his voice in song
he brought his brothers into chorus
with a deep and wondrous chant.
Evening blessed his bones
and sleep swept him up in dreams
of temples and of stones.
Encouraged by his second find,
he knew a holy third was not far off.

* * *

His journey now led through Galilee
to caverns of the sacred hills,
with monasteries filled with jars of words.
He felt his find was waiting there.
Brothers asked,
"And what seeketh thee?"
He replied,
"The orb of visions casts a personal glow
and when it's found I shall know."
Nodding, understanding heads
bowed to shared meals
and the delight of muted conversations
feeding hungry souls.
Juan read and read and yet was not moved
by what he found.
While deep in meditation he asked,
"Is it here, Lord?"
An answer came silently as a whisper
in the wind,
"No."
Although late in the evening,
he took his staff and bidding his fellows
blessed times,
left again for trails towards the rising sun
where Persia beckoned beyond hills of rock
and sand
and roads led to great rivers.
Through desert and through mountains
days were spent in cadenced prayer,
as footsteps took him deeper and deeper
into solitude.
There,
the grandeur and expanse of God's face
presented smiles and wrinkles
always pleasing to his eyes.

He wandered past nomads and their flocks
and thanking his God for Muslim hospitality,
graciously shared conversations
of the beauty of the Quran.
Then,
when they knelt and bowed in prayer
as hours struck their due,
he would likewise kneel
with inclined head in silent prayer.
Often wonderings blossomed
from the scenes of bent forms
facing Holy Mecca,
meeting obligations
in prayerful repetitions.
How wonderful it was to see
his brothers' dedications
to sharing selves with God.
They with their beads and he with his,
litanies of man's journeys to the Throne.
And so were spent the days and weeks
before arriving in Baghdad.
Seeking repose with brothers of the Crescent
he took refuge in a mosque
and fell to reading studies from the scriptures.
With shoulders bent and mind illumined,
he spent months in travels of heart and mind.
As was his custom,
upon entering a new relationship with a scroll,
he would bow his head and pray
that there within
he would find another lucent stone.
And there it was!

That magnificent, flowing script
in the margin of a copy of a study on
the Eternal.
Intuition beyond doubt,
the yesing of the ages laid bare
in the language of the soul.
As the call to prayers echoed from the minaret,
he bowed in deep thanksgiving
and preparation for his task.
After kneeling in reverent, sharing silence,
he went quietly to the desk of his cell
and taking out his rolled parchment,
he gently untied its thong
and unrolled the precious record of his finds.
Setting flat stones on three corners,
the other held down with his hand,
and taking the stylus
he wrote his find.
"Yabe! / Yabo! – Me! / Yome!"
True! / Not true! Mine! / Not Mine!
"And in so being,
Yours and everyone's!"
he added in reflective prayer.
The clerics and imams were pleased
that sharing had helped a fellow soul towards
its seeking of Allah,
the Compassionate,
the Merciful,
and in so doing creating a
deepening understanding of the whole.
Again,
he thanked his fellow brothers
for their help and gracious hospitality.

And in leaving he said,
"Allah,
the Compassionate,
the Merciful,
brought me down this path and you gave me
water, food, and shelter.
May Allah,
the Compassionate,
the Merciful,
hold you in his heart."
Having uttered his thanksgiving,
he again took up his staff and left for
Arabia.
His Muslim brothers had shown him
that men of different faiths
could share presence
when mutual respect was had by all.
As he placed his feet once more upon the trails
of his times,
he wondered why in peace
there could be such deep and wonderful sharing,
while in war the unreasoned mind,
bent upon destruction,
pillaged, burned, and brutalized
the neighbors of yesterday and tomorrow.
History's paths had proven fickle
when confronted with the strength of commerce,
the mundane,
and mammon became a god.
As sandals dutifully carried him to new lands,
his mind reflected upon
the wisdom of the scrolls.
"Such waves of thought sweep the sea of man,"
he thought.
"What purpose in creating so many divergent positions
on the face of creation?"
Musings led him to fasting and to prayer.

He murmured,
"There are always so many,
always so much.
Was there a lodestone that weighed enough,
or a mirror
in which all there was to see
could then be seen?"
With a mix of adoration and wonder,
Juan de Aragon wound his way
through the sands of Arabia to Medina.
And there,
in that Holy place,
was again invited to stay with his brothers
while he continued to search the archives
for his stones.
In reading the studies of the Quran
and the ancillary texts that positioned
holy documents in the context of their time,
he was intrigued by the aspect of war
and proselytizing that was contained
in the studies.
He came to see that there was
a concomitant circumstance,
an *other side* to the coin of war.
It was an omnipresence of essential movement,
for some a conversion toward
a manifestation
of one's acquired faith.
As he worked through the documents
he began to see
an immediacy of action, advocated
in adherence to the laws of Islam.
"As there should be
in any faith's commitment
to its stated objectives,"
he thought.

And yet there was that sense of nowness
that kept appearing in the documents.
And so it was that he came to feel
this was indeed another stone.
Moving to the bench
he again took the now tattered-edged parchment
from his tunic and lifting stylus to ink well
set it to task writing his fourth word.
"Ya neh!"
Understood to be Now!
After all, wasn't this the focus of all life:
To own its presence in its current interface
with the surrounds of the moment?
The Greeks in their literature spoke of existence
as a prima facie state of being for all being.
Was this not the touching of the Divine
as Presence of Being
was made manifest in its sharing?
Juan de Aragon reflected upon the many mandates
of time in the Muslim faith,
leaving each and every act
not between a now and then
but always in the now,
presenting a path to yet another now
which was always a present now.
He had admired the logicians
of the Greek and Muslim literary traditions
as they maintained their fidelity to an existentialism,
that for him
had become a holy pastime.
To stay in a field of prayer,
always maintaining an understanding
of the purpose of one's own being,
in returning the magnificence of one's gifts
to any and all others
as time unfolds in its eternal now,
was life itself.

As in the past,
when Juan de Aragon found a new stone,
he would thank his brothers
for their gracious hospitality and take his leave
to begin again his unfinished journey
to place in context the stones
for a temple to his God.

* * *

His path
led him back to the caves of Judea
and to an old monastery above the shores
of the Dead Sea.
The silence of the desert with its rich aesthetics
never stopped amazing him.
From the forests of the Pyrenees
to the swamps along the rivers of Persia,
he never stopped marveling
at the richness of the Divine Plan:
to grace each and every place
with a beauty of deep and profound significance.
He thought,
"This is an integral part of God's Plan –
to surprise us in every way at every place."
It must have been,
because he certainly was,
and the accolades of the scribes
attested to the fact
with an abundance of recordings
on the magnificence of nature.
Between lengthy sessions of reading
in the archives
he would take long serene walks in the desert
to place in context
the stones of his journey.
He now had four and with them felt confident
that others would see their profound significance.

As he reflected
and faced the Cardinal Points
he repeated each and every one over and over
in the form of a chant.
As each new one was added
they began to roll from his deep chest
in the form of bold song,
"One!
Still!
True!
Now!"
He kept repeating them over and over
adding each one as his journey continued
and as he said his daily prayers.
If, indeed,
they were to form the foundation
to a temple of the divinity of being,
they must be made a part
of everyone's waking hours
as they sought to spend their time
in service to the All.
They, slowly like a growing thing,
began to develop a harmonious mass.
They came to represent a hymn
resonating with his very sense of being.
And it was then that yet again,
in searching through cracked and broken
pieces of parchment,
he stumbled upon a common phrase,
and it appeared to him to be truly seen
for the first time.
Hurrying to the writing tables,
afraid that the significance would be lost again
among the commonness of other words,
he took out and unrolled his parchment,
then with stylus penned his fifth word:

"Amanth!"
Love!
That is, to love one another.
Love means
that seemingly unconditional act
of communion with all things.
It sets them apart to be revered,
to become an intimate part of one's own soul.
Love is an act of self-coincidence
whispering to the ear of the soul
as its will snaps to attention
as if it is of the utmost importance,
or better yet feelings surging from,
merging with and permeating
one's very own being.
Love is a recipe for drinking from life's
full goblet or chalice,
a cup that truly runneth over
with joys and fulfillments of being.
Whenever it is present
there is a surrounding halo
consuming those who feel its touch.
Yet it is much more than words
and much more than touch.
It is just as it should be,
Truth Itself.
Reveling in his fifth find,
he again bid farewell to his brothers
and taking his staff, departed
towards the high mountains of India.
There it was told that
ancient writings abounded of man's search
for a relationship to self,
to purpose,
and to God.

* * *

With renewed vigor and steps accompanying
his holy chant,
he went upon his way.
His wonderings were washed with thoughts
of his precious stones.
In the sharing of them,
he supposed others would be moved
to a universal understanding,
leading to a profound peace,
squelching all songs and cries of war.
"What was it that was needed
in the minds of men
that would cause such a realization,
transforming their actions
from war to peace?"
Lost in these ponderings,
he crossed the great rivers,
greeting each rising of the sun with refreshed hope,
knowing in his mind that his journey
was one that, once completed, would provide
an opportunity for all men
to stand and say,
Yes!
Yes! to the sameness of their yearnings
and the needs of all the children.
And in saying this,
he reflected upon the role of women
in the great hierarchy of the Divine Plan.
They must have some grand purpose
and must be deserving of manifold respect
in their holding presences of life and purpose.
There had been times in his travels
when he had seen a sadness upon their faces
and had sensed a longing in their hearts.

He had often wondered if it was a longing
for their children,
their daughters
in their lives of subjugation,
or was this a dedication to a purpose
that was beyond a man's ability to comprehend?
And yet,
as always,
his mind was brought back to the fact
of his own dear mother.
The breasts of life,
the touch of a loving hand,
the sound of a loving voice.
He could not be shaken from the thought
of the Divine's loving touch
in such a magnificent example
of His creation.
It was this
that he bore in mind
as he spent his many evenings
in reflective repose and prayer.
He reasoned that all women,
each and every one from child to adult,
were deserving of protection and respect.
With these mullings
and with the resonance of his holy chant,
he arrived upon the slopes of the Himalayas.
Here he was treated to the cymbals
and dervishes
of a deeply sensitive culture.
Asking for a man of wisdom,
he was led to a Teacher.
He asked to be informed in the ancient writings
and knowledge of the people.

It was thus that he was introduced to the songs
and poetry of the traveling sages
and the myths and legends
of their trials and tribulations
as they strove to order their world
and make sense of Nature's plan.
As he listened and began to find paths
to the depths of these wonderfully industrious people,
he marveled at their purposeful activity.
There was,
when the yesness of the soul was owned,
a brilliant flash of being
illuminating the surrounds,
sending vibrations that enveloped
one in All and all in One.
He reflected upon the many mystical paths
recorded over time,
and how glowing souls
had shared their insights with others.
Knowing full well that an insight was personal,
and yet to be a person
was what each and every one of us
was about.
It then came to him –
the sixth word.
Again taking the stylus and parchment
for the sixth time, he wrote,
from the ancient Sutras,
"Matisu!"
Growth!
He reasoned that
to grow is to grow into awareness,
an awareness of being a witness.
To grow is to witness.

To witness
is to come into contact
with that which is always already there,
and yet it is something that we must come to know,
we must grow into it.
We must become it,
because it is who we really are.
To be one's own real self
is to grow into our one real self.
He danced for joy,
having seen his fellow brothers,
the wisdom seekers,
dance in the sheer joy of being,
he took to the air with his body
and his feet flew about under him
as his arms waved through the very air of being.
He had grown from a staid man
to an open being.
One who was able to maintain a fidelity
to his personhood
and still incorporate the magnificence
of the rest of being.
"I am more of me now that I have met you!"
he said with joy
as he danced and danced,
whirling about, waving his entire body
in the sheer joy of being in touch
with the All.
He knew he had grown in his journey
in finding what he had come to call his stones.

* * *

Then,
once again he thanked his many teachers
for their presence of being in the lives of others
and in their willingness to share their being
with him.

To share is to love,
to love is to know.
Once again he reflected upon those key words
of the process of being a person:
to know,
to care,
to be responsible,
to respect,
to be in contact with the real in himself
that was the real in another.
He would now return to his home abbey
and share what he had learned with his brothers.
He knew sharing would take time,
time to understand,
time to practice,
time to grow.
His return took him along the southern belly
of the steppes.
Wandering the well-trodden trails
of the many migrations of people
who had come as waves of the great human sea,
he thought of the apparent differences that motivated them
to follow,
to conquer,
to stay,
to take and to become with the preexisting
while adding their drop to the great boiling stew of humanity.
Always different,
always the same.
Men and women,
children and more life.
It was as it had always been.
"Why was there the suffering in between?"
he asked his God.
"Because there is that which must be as it is
and as it must choose to become.

To each is their path.
I have made it so."
He stopped at a monastery
overlooking the Iron Gates,
gates that could not hold the hordes,
but that funneled and mixed the stew
as it flowed through the loins of the earth
on its way to its tomorrows,
our tomorrows,
all those tomorrows of our forever.
Thus forcing the whole
to grow into an awareness
that all was Holy.
Every parchment he read from the dusty shelves
and the confluence of the ages kept saying
the same thing,
"All is Holy!"
And so it was that Juan de Aragon
took for the seventh and last time
his parchment from his tunic.
Then, sitting at a bench and leaning over a table
used by Christian and by Muslim,
he wrote the last stone:
"Alhelig!"
All Is Holy!
He rolled the scroll and tied its thong,
placing it again next to his heart.
Then he mounted the stairs to the parapet
and strolled along its ancient ramparts,
chanting in his resonating voice:
"One ... Still ... True ...
Now ... Love ...
Growth ...
Holy ...
Growth ...
Love ... Now ...
True ... Still ... One ..."

Every wave of successive humanity
had brought with it gifts
with which to share their creative genius
for wanting to push ever further
into the realms
of God's creation.
And to follow in the footsteps
of those who had gone before.
This coiling up and cresting of migrations
was his last *stone*.
"The last shall be first,
and the first shall be last."
And so it was, and so it is.
The ancient prayer that Socrates had recalled
before drinking the hemlock,
"As it was in the beginning, is now,
and forever shall be,"
rang across the valley,
carried on the mistlettes of the evening's breath.
Bells tolled from belfries.
Imams called from minarets.
The day was closing upon itself.
All was well in the world.

* * *

On his way to Rome
Juan reflected,
"Whether patrician, plebe, or slave, it mattered not."
Great movements of humanity
had come together to build and to destroy
and to build again.
It all became a flowing Divine River
crashing upon and slipping along new shores.

"**One** ... **Still** ... **True** ...
Now ... **Love** ...
Growth ...
Holy."

As he approached the ancient city,
he thought being a person,
serving one's own love for self,
for others, and for God,
did not have to be any grand theological system,
although there was a need to know
some of the steps of humanity's path.
Life demands a constant effort.
One could not touch the Sacred
in any way other than a sacred way.
It would have to be from that deep well of
yeses
that gushes from all of the fountains
of truth that ever flowed, were flowing now,
or would ever flow.
There was no need to guess
from the morass of human ponderings.
One could,
by being honest with the steps others had taken,
ascertain whether they had satisfied
their commitment to themselves,
their brothers, and their sisters.
And whether their lives were lived
in that sacred space
of complementing
what was already theirs and there.
As he reflected on the stones
he envisioned a circle,
an elevated bridge that took one
into the garden of humanity and across time,
giving all a sense of belonging,
a belonging that pulled from the depths of one
the gift of love.
A gift that could be shared with each
and every thing
in the garden of creation.

He musingly smiled,
realizing it did not matter if a choice was made
to go straight or in circles.
The curving bridge could be
large or small
depending upon the force of
one's willingness to seek
and to follow their commitment.
It was indeed self-coincidental integrity,
allowing each and every one
to own their participation
in the process of creation.
After all,
God's mansion was large,
full of infinite manifestations
of love.
The pine loved itself enough
to present the world with cones of many seeds,
most of which
would not become pine trees.
They would,
as with all trees and other plants and animals,
forever live a holy dedication to themselves
and to the great sea of creation
flowing through the earth
and Heaven.
As with all
of Nature's efficient abundance,
it is always a
"Yes!"

THE BRIDGE
(A HOLY CIRCLE)

** Play ONE! **
**

Stand STILL   All is a HOLY Endeavor
in Silence to See!   Follow All the Stones!
**   *******
*******   **
TRUE! / Not True!   Dedicate Oneself
Mine! / Not Mine!   to GROWTH!
***   ******
******   ***
Own It NOW!   Act in LOVE!
****   *****
*****   ****

www.ingramcontent.com/pod-product-compliance
Lightning Source LLC
Chambersburg PA
CBHW022304060426
42446CB00007BA/583